S0-BCW-505

DISNEY's
HOW · TO · DRAW

THE LITTLE
MERMAID

Illustrated by
Philo Barnhart
Diana Wakeman

Walter Foster

The Making of *The Little Mermaid*

After the overwhelming success of *Snow White and the Seven Dwarfs*, Walt Disney immediately began work on a number of new projects, one of which was *The Little Mermaid*. This moving story of courage and love seemed a natural for animation. Preliminary story sketches were made, but work was halted with the outbreak of World War II. It wasn't until 1986 that the Disney Studios again turned its attention to the plight of Hans Christian Andersen's little mermaid.

The Little Mermaid featured more underwater action than any previous Disney film. The artists soon learned that the movement, weight, and speed of the characters were directly influenced by their watery environment. Hundreds of iridescent bubbles, gently waving seaweed, and brilliant tropical

fish made King Triton's kingdom the most fabulous ever designed. Authentic details on Prince Eric's ship and a magnificent castle by the sea show the care taken to ensure that *The Little Mermaid* would become another animation classic.

The huge success of *The Little Mermaid* is largely due to the careful development of each of its characters. From Ariel's pert chin to Sebastian's drooping eyelids, no detail was overlooked.

Ariel's character was developed by studying a wide variety of human and cartoon models.

In order to get an idea of what Ariel should look like, Disney artists scoured hundreds of magazines looking for a face that was fresh, young, and appealing. There were discussions about whether Ariel should be glamorous and exotic or cute and athletic. Part of the research included a review of past Disney heroines. Ariel is most similar to Alice (from *Alice in Wonderland*) in appearance. Both have a large forehead, long, loose hair, wide-set eyes, and a small mouth and chin.

The non-human characters gave the artists an even broader range of ideas with which to work. The character of Ursula the Sea Witch was originally designed as a mermaid. She was then given an eel's tail. But after

Alice

Ariel

Even in the earliest sketches, Ursula's wicked nature was apparent.

viewing a film of an octopus moving across the ocean floor, the Disney artists knew they had found the right way to express Ursula's extravagant personality. As for Sebastian, his deep voice and melodramatic statements seemed all the more humorous coming from a tiny crab. And Scuttle the seagull's dark eyebrows and expressive round eyes were based closely on those of the man who gave him voice, Buddy Hackett.

Drawing Techniques

Drawing Ariel and her friends can be fun and rewarding. With a little patience and practice, you will soon be producing successful drawings of your own.

Most characters are based on simple round and oval shapes. Using a light, continuous motion, sketch around and around until you've made a circle or oval that is the correct shape. Also practice drawing curves with smooth strokes. You may then erase any stray lines for a clean look. Try sketching a variety of sizes, or join shapes together to create new shapes.

Most Disney characters are drawn with a ball for the head and a line of action showing the direction of the body. This line gives your character movement and life. It should flow naturally and smoothly.

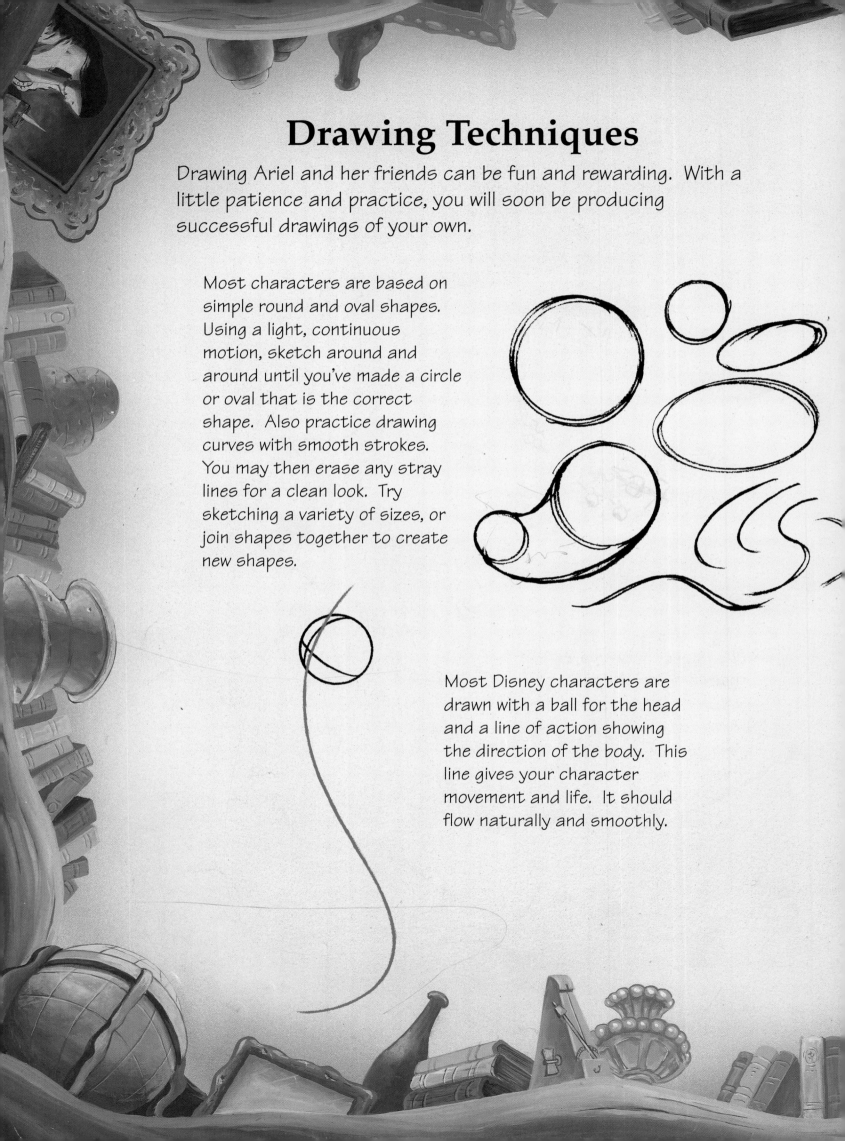

It's useful to transfer the outline of your drawing onto tracing paper. This gives you a silhouette that reflects the character's proportions and shows if you have created a clear, strong pose. A good silhouette leads to a good finished drawing.

Once you've drawn your character, carefully erase the line of action and other construction lines to clean up your drawing. Now you're ready to color Ariel.

Ariel's Head

The three-quarter view is the best angle to use to make a character look three-dimensional. Notice how much depth, form, and structure can be achieved in this drawing.

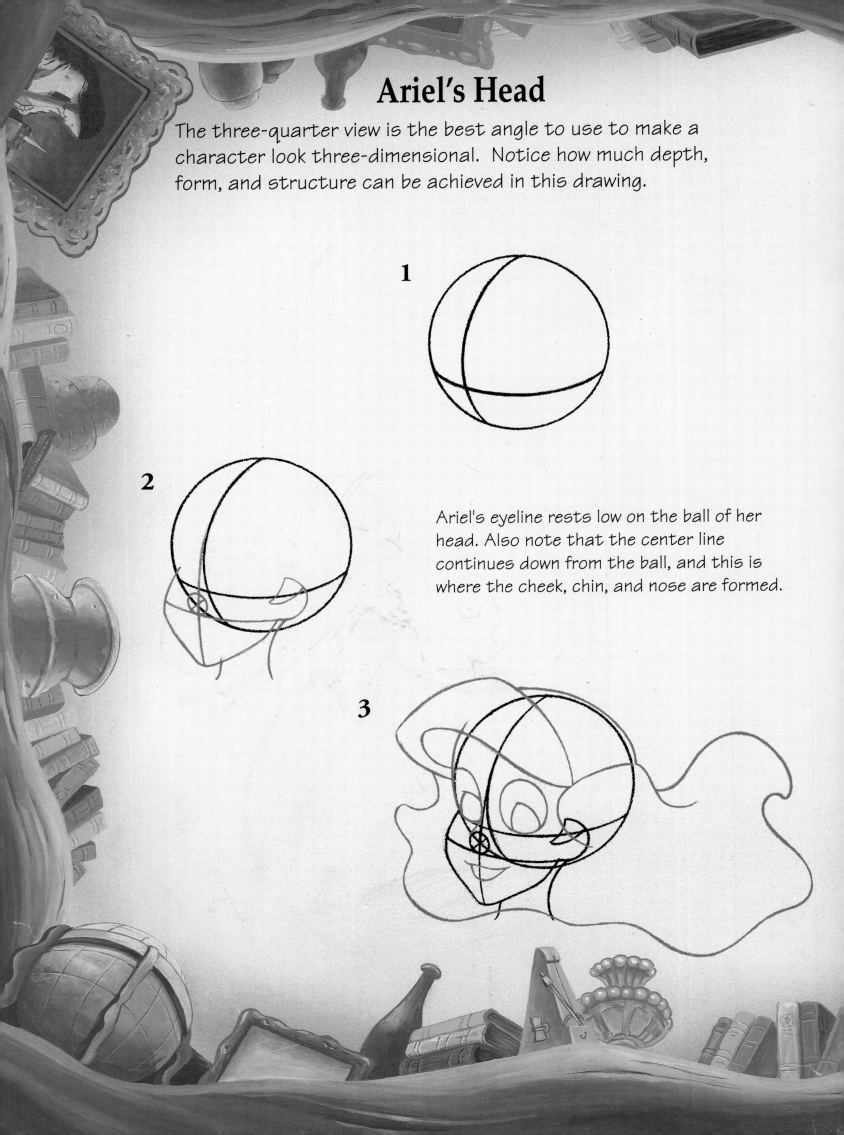

1

2

Ariel's eyeline rests low on the ball of her head. Also note that the center line continues down from the ball, and this is where the cheek, chin, and nose are formed.

3

4

5

6

Ariel's Expressions

Knowing the attitude you would like to portray can make the character more believable. Even though expressions create shape changes in Ariel's face, the head volume remains the same.

determined

daydreaming

enchanted

happy

surprised

concerned

amused

Ariel Three-Quarter View

People around the world have been charmed by Ariel's cheerful enthusiasm. Be sure to show some of her energy when drawing her complete figure.

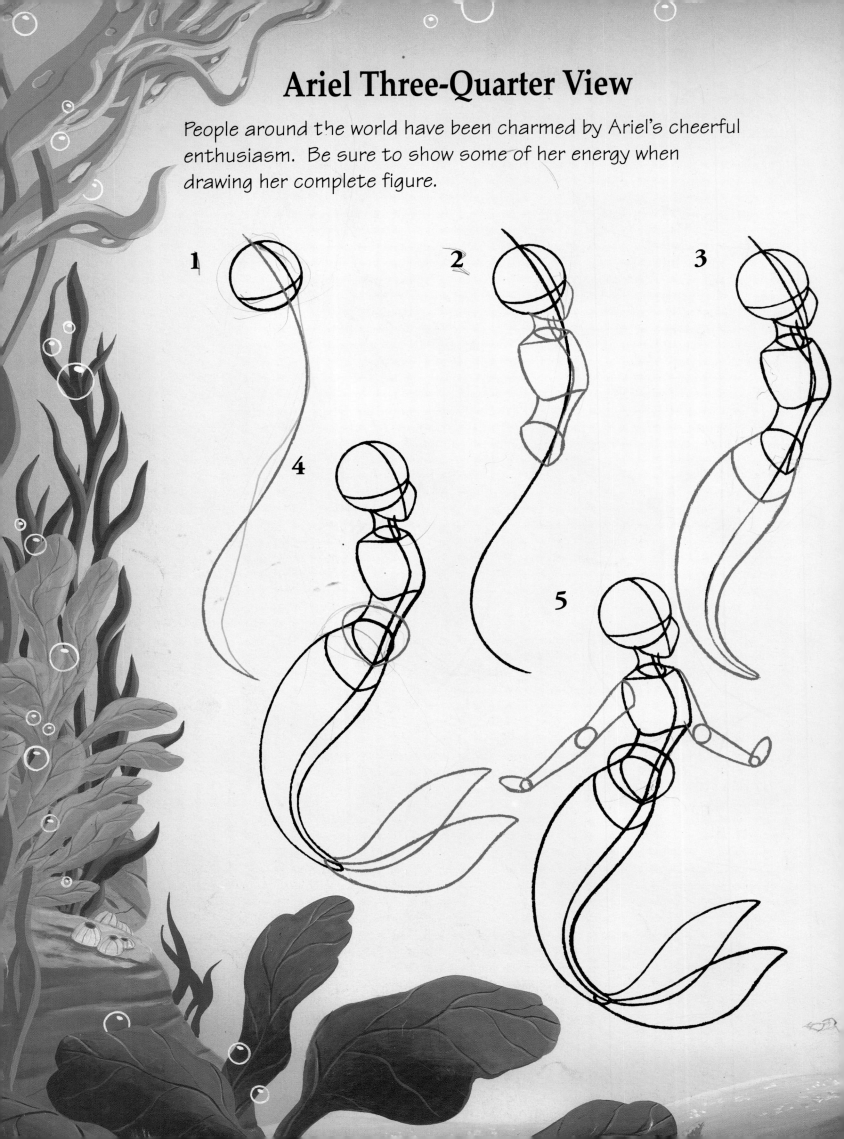

6

7

8

A strong line of action will help give the feeling that Ariel's body flows naturally into her graceful tail.

Ariel Action Poses

Ariel's personality, mannerisms, and charm all come to life with the right action poses. Practice drawing the poses illustrated and then create some new ones of your own.

Sebastian

Sebastian is a little crab with a big voice and a big heart, as well. Try to bring out the warmer side of his personality when drawing him.

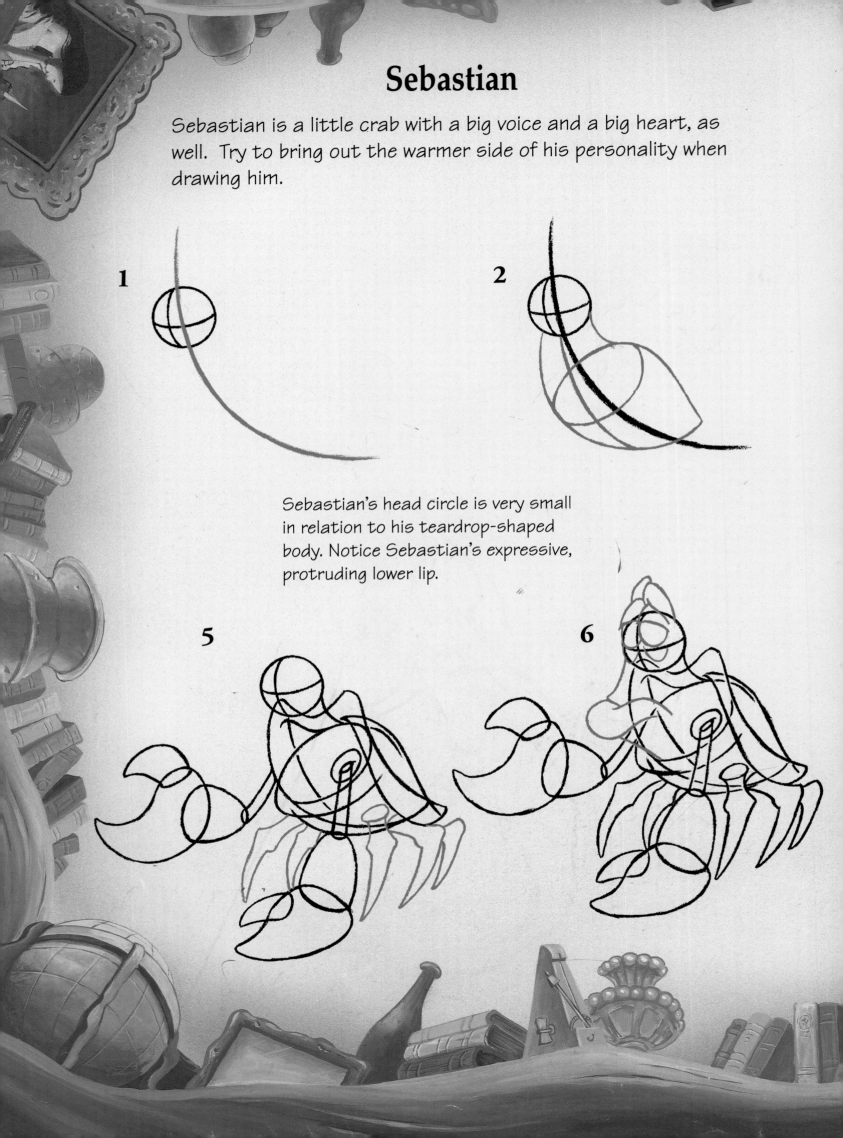

1

2

Sebastian's head circle is very small in relation to his teardrop-shaped body. Notice Sebastian's expressive, protruding lower lip.

5

6

Sebastian's Poses and Expressions

When drawing Sebastian in action, notice that his hard shell does not change shape. It is his flexible face that can be exaggerated to show movement. Try this squash-and-stretch technique when drawing Sebastian in action.

happy

showing off

fearful

proud

doubtful

singing

bowing

Flounder Three-Quarter View

Flounder's spunk and vulnerability are the qualities that make him so memorable. Use this three-quarter view to show all the depth of his chubby cheeks and oval nose.

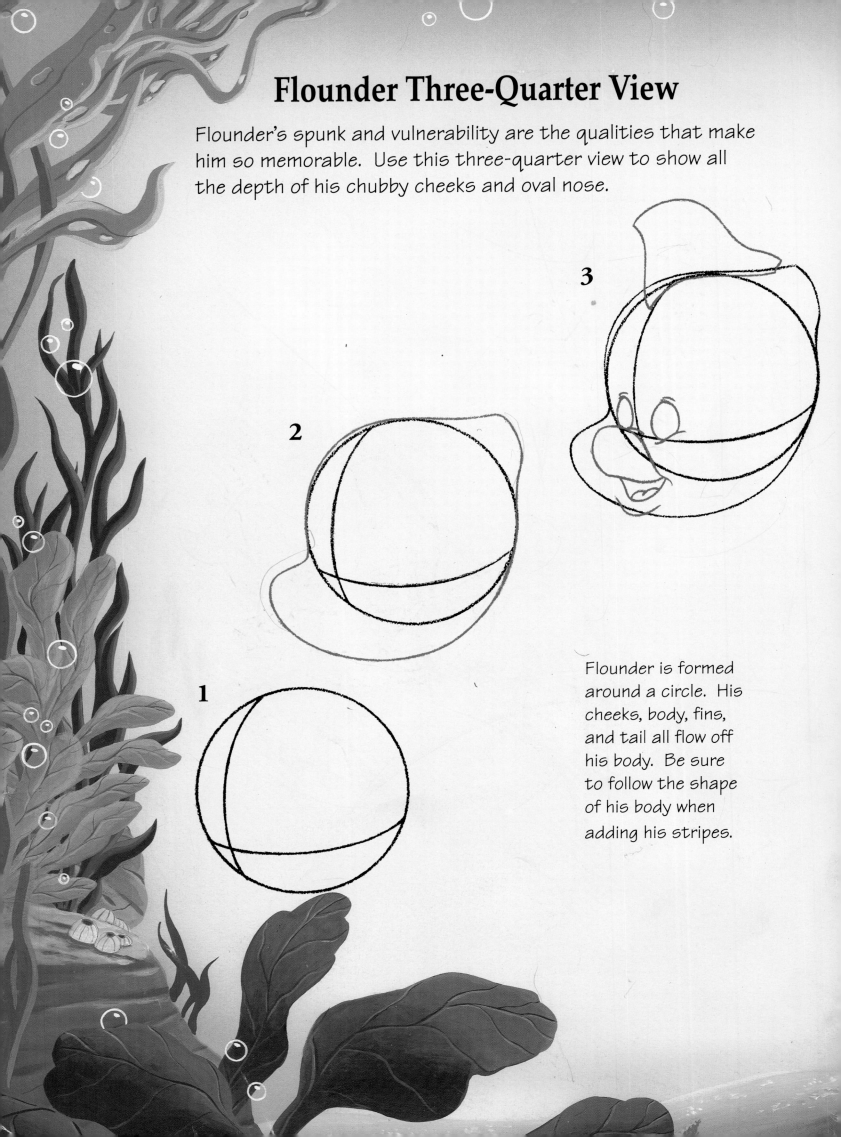

Flounder is formed around a circle. His cheeks, body, fins, and tail all flow off his body. Be sure to follow the shape of his body when adding his stripes.

4

5

6

Flounder's Poses and Expressions

Since Flounder doesn't have any limbs to draw, he is limited to simple arcs of action. However, his face can show a wide variety of emotions. Here are some of the different ways he can be drawn.

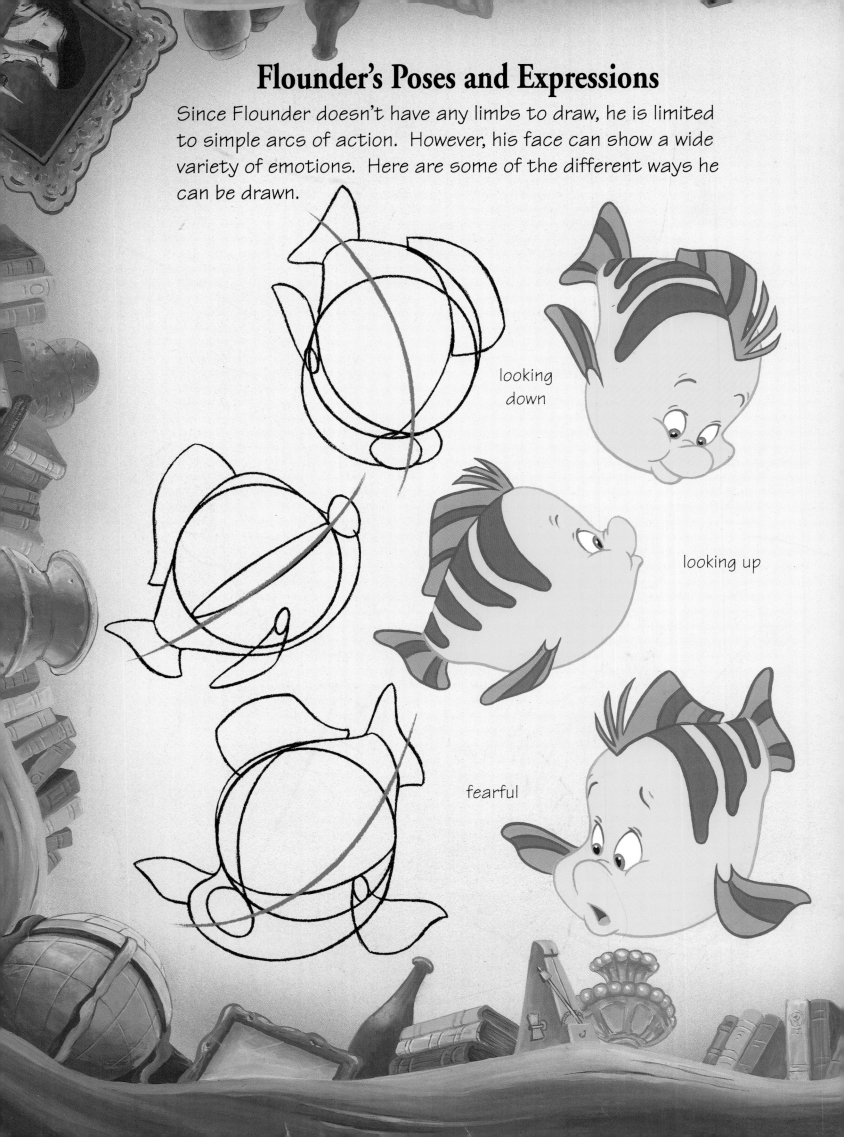

looking down

looking up

fearful

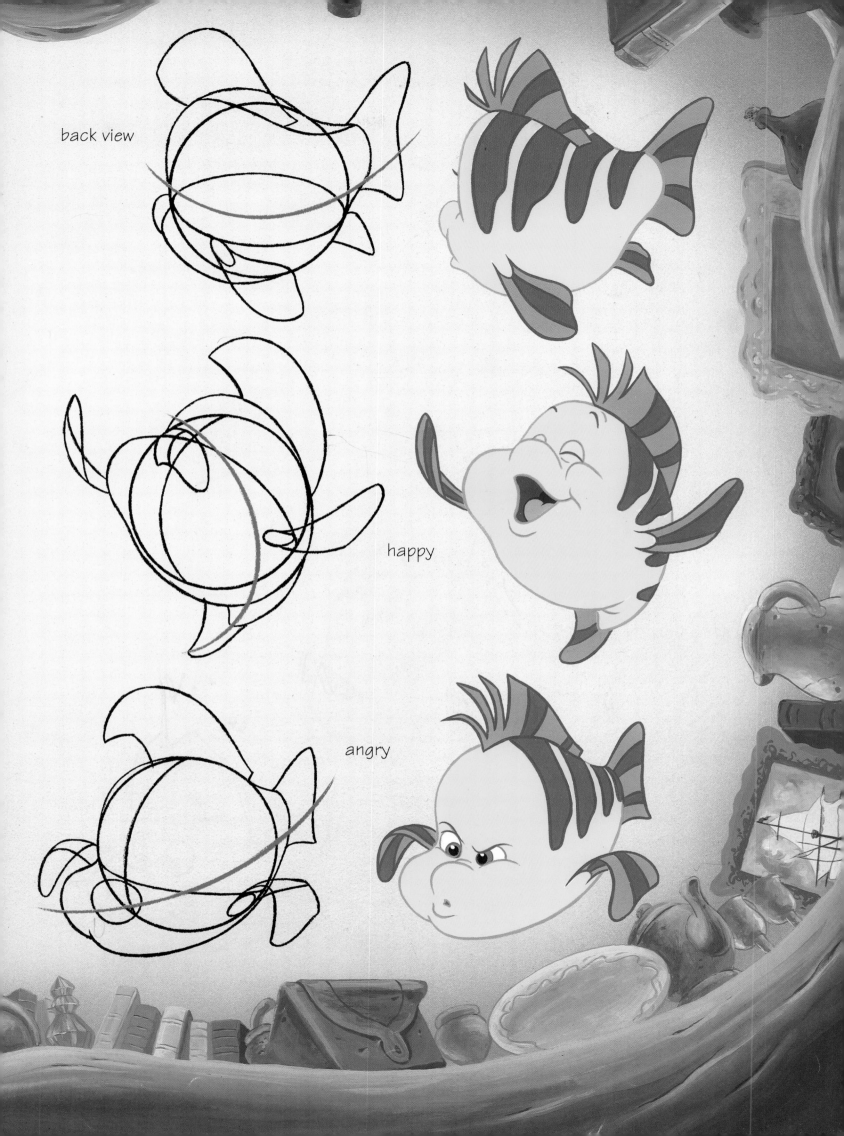

back view

happy

angry

Ursula's Head

This three-quarter view of Ursula's head shows the depth of her full face. Her flame-like hair shapes and frames her face and suggests her evil mind. See if you can capture her diabolical personality.

Although Ursula's head is small, but her jawline is very wide. Angular ovals create her eyes and eyebrows.

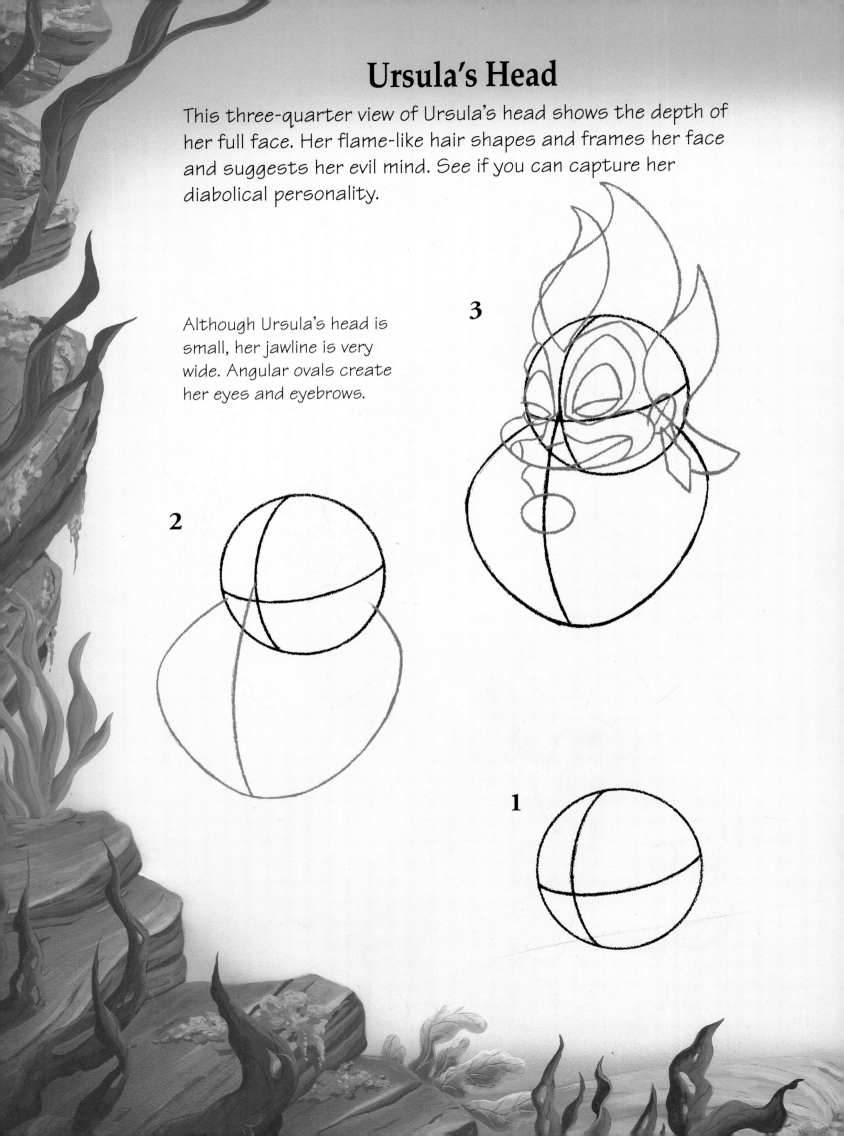

4

5

6

Don't forget Ursula's beauty mark.

Ursula Three-Quarter View

Ursula is basically constructed of simple shapes. Her six legs can be used either to propel her or to act as extra arms. All six are not always visible.

The top half of Ursula's body is smaller and more angular than the bottom half.

6

The legs should
appear to
join together
underneath
Ursula's wide body.

7

Ursula's Poses and Expressions

Ursula's gestures and expressions are dramatic and exaggerated. She is composed of circular shapes that you can squash and stretch to animate her.

furious

fearful

joyful

greedy

scheming

conniving

Scuttle's Head

Scuttle the sea gull is a lovable, goofy character. His full cheeks and long beak are best viewed in a three-quarter pose.

1

2

Draw Scuttle with full, feathery cheeks. His long beak has a teardrop shape at the end.

3

6

Scuttle's eyes are usually crossed, and he has thick, dark eyebrows.

5

4

Scuttle Standing

Scuttle is overweight and scruffy. Now that you have learned to draw his head, you can move on to drawing his full body.

1

2

Scuttle's back is a concave curve, while his chest and lower body protrude in a convex curve.

3

Scuttle's Poses and Expressions

Scuttle's wings can imitate the action of human arms and fingers in very broad moves. Try the squash-and-stretch technique on his face and body to animate him even more.

flying

thoughtful

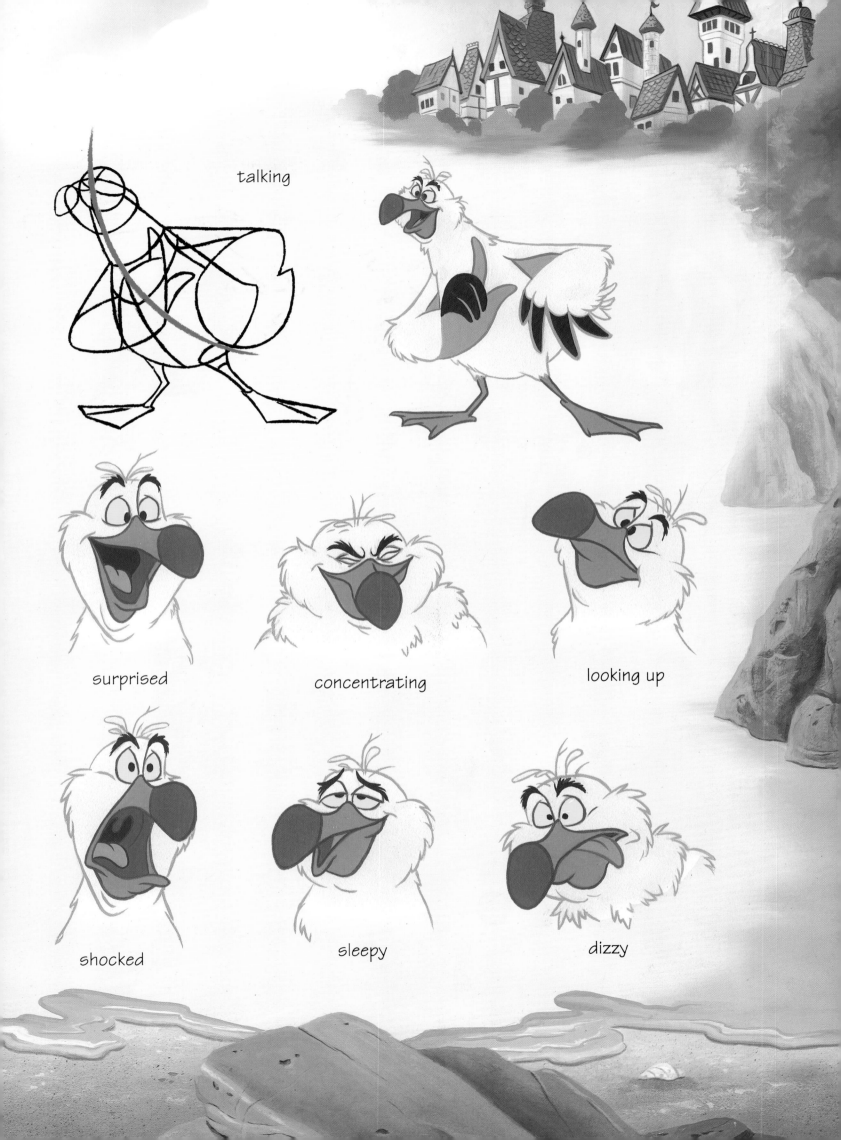

talking

surprised

concentrating

looking up

shocked

sleepy

dizzy

Eric's Head

Of all the characters from *The Little Mermaid*, Eric's proportions are closest to those of an actual human. Here's how to draw his face.

1

Eric has a strong, angular jaw and chinline.

2

3

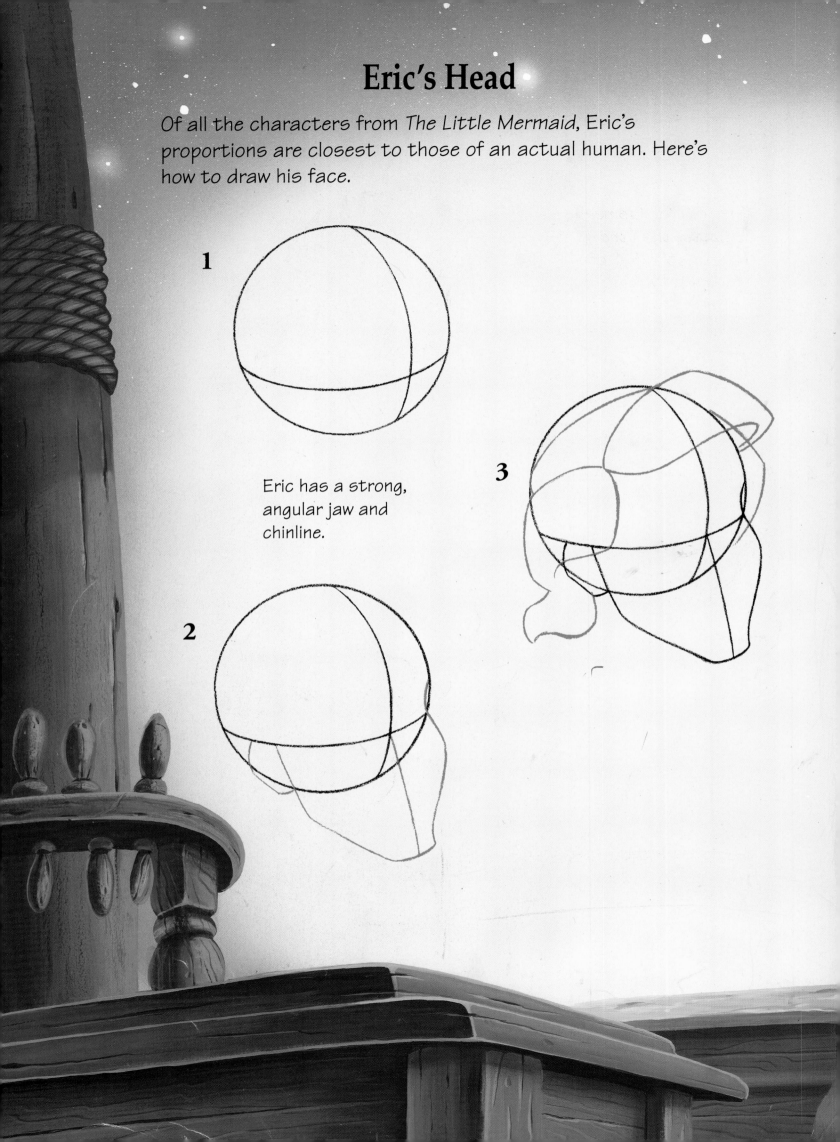

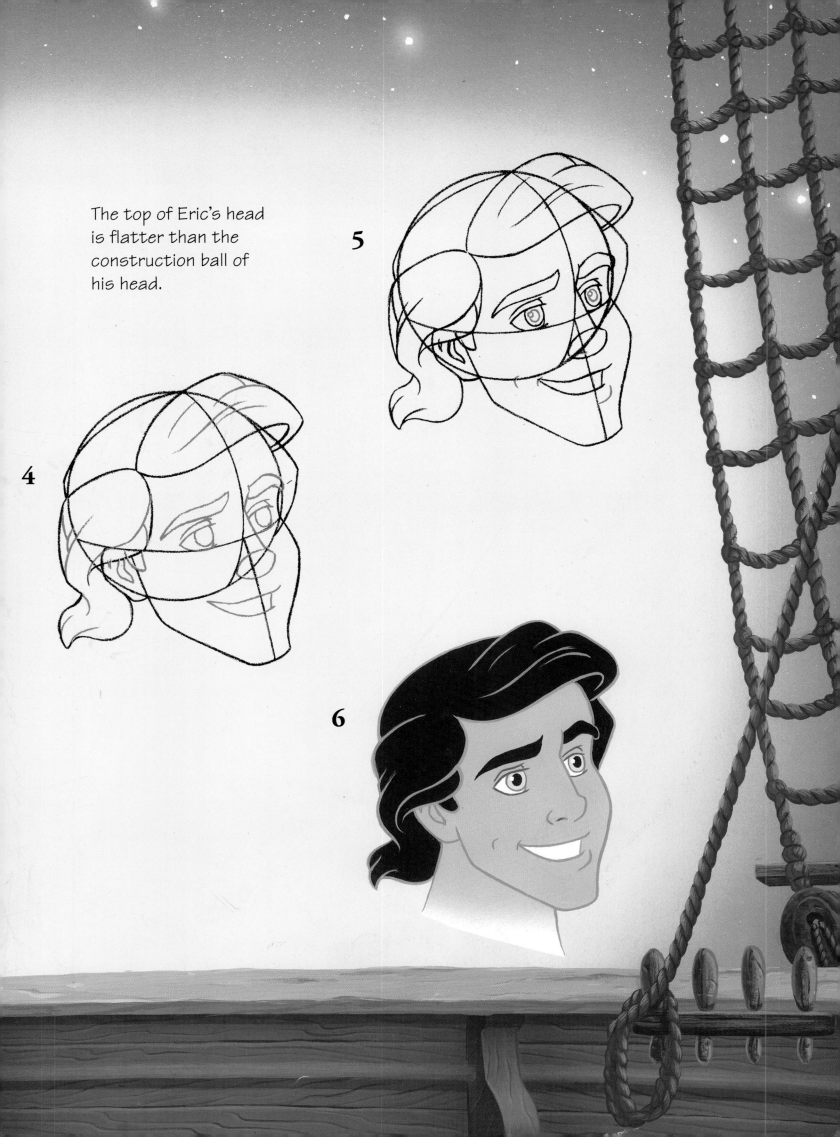

The top of Eric's head is flatter than the construction ball of his head.

5

4

6

Eric Standing

After you have practiced drawing Eric's head and face, you are ready to move on to his body. He's a prince, so be sure he stands proudly.

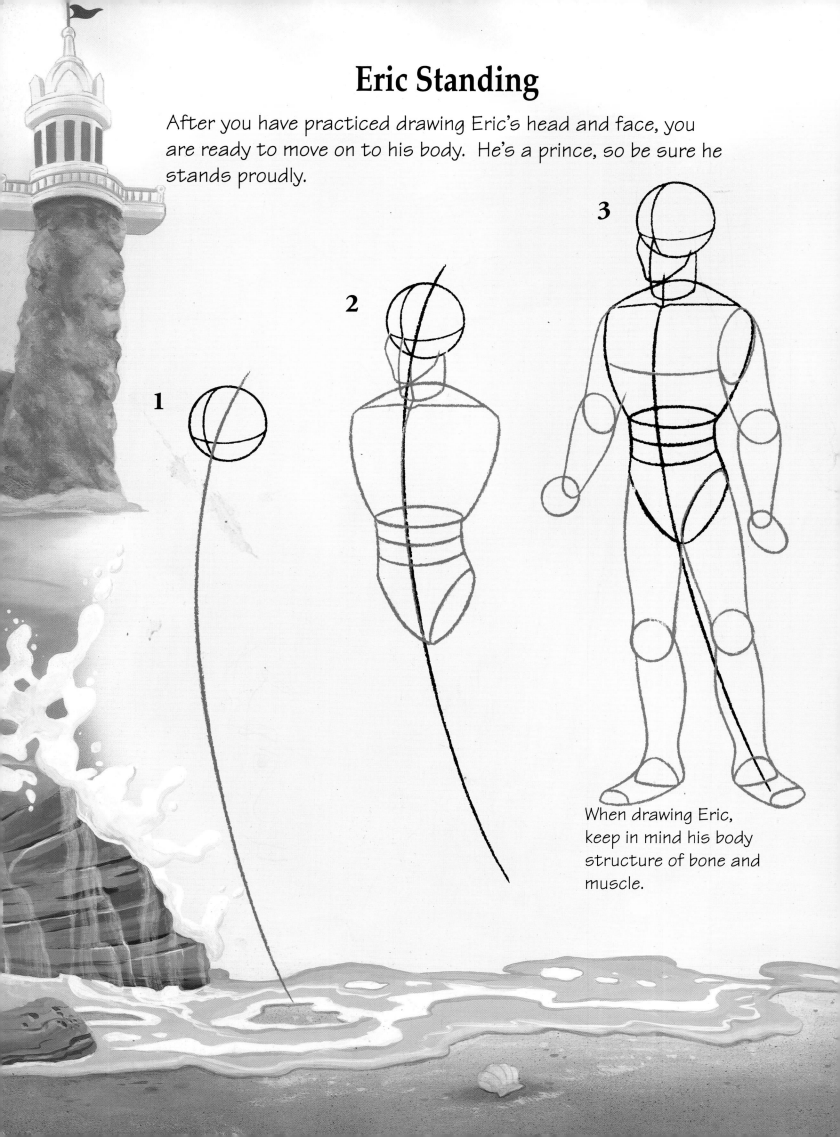

When drawing Eric, keep in mind his body structure of bone and muscle.

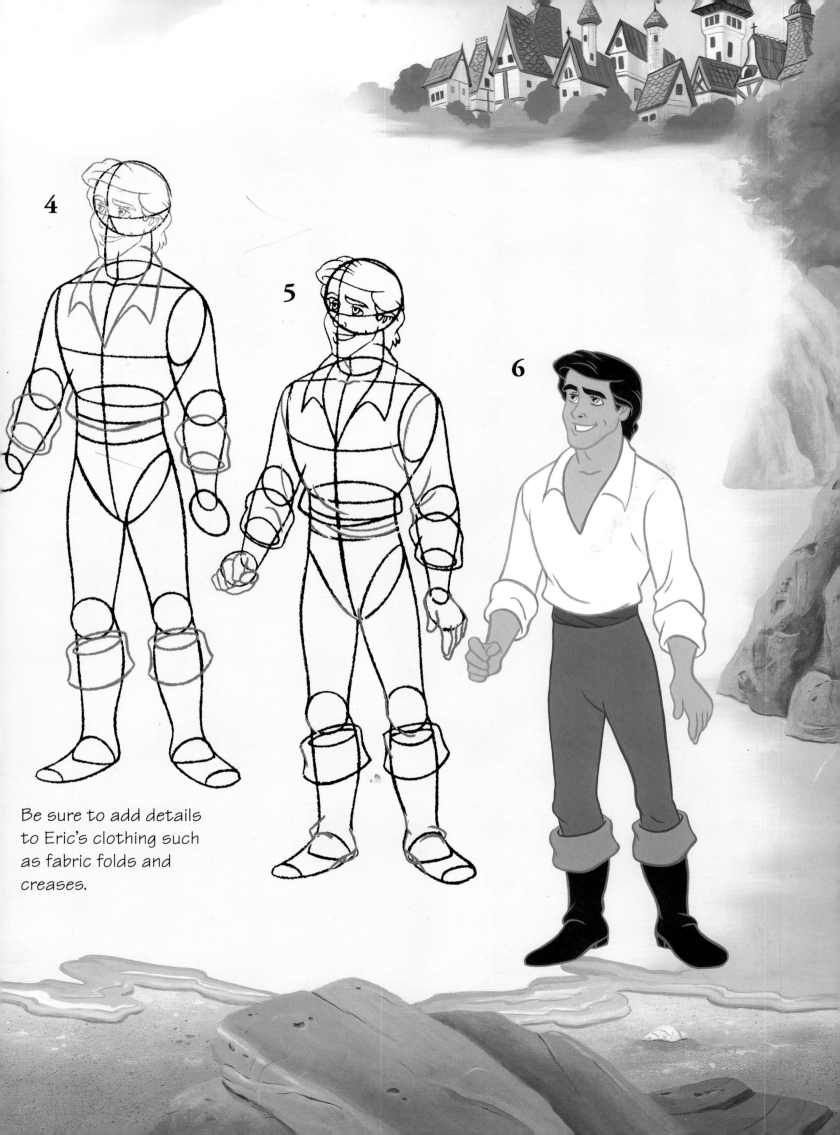

4

5

6

Be sure to add details to Eric's clothing such as fabric folds and creases.

Eric's Poses and Expressions

Eric is a strong, athletic prince who loves the high seas. Try showing his different expressions when drawing him in these action poses.

surprised

daydreaming

angry

thoughtful

confused

Secondary Characters

Secondary characters play an important role in enriching the storyline and setting. The only difference between Flotsam and Jetsam is that Flotsam's yellow eye is on the right, Jetsam's is on the left.

King Triton

Chef Louie

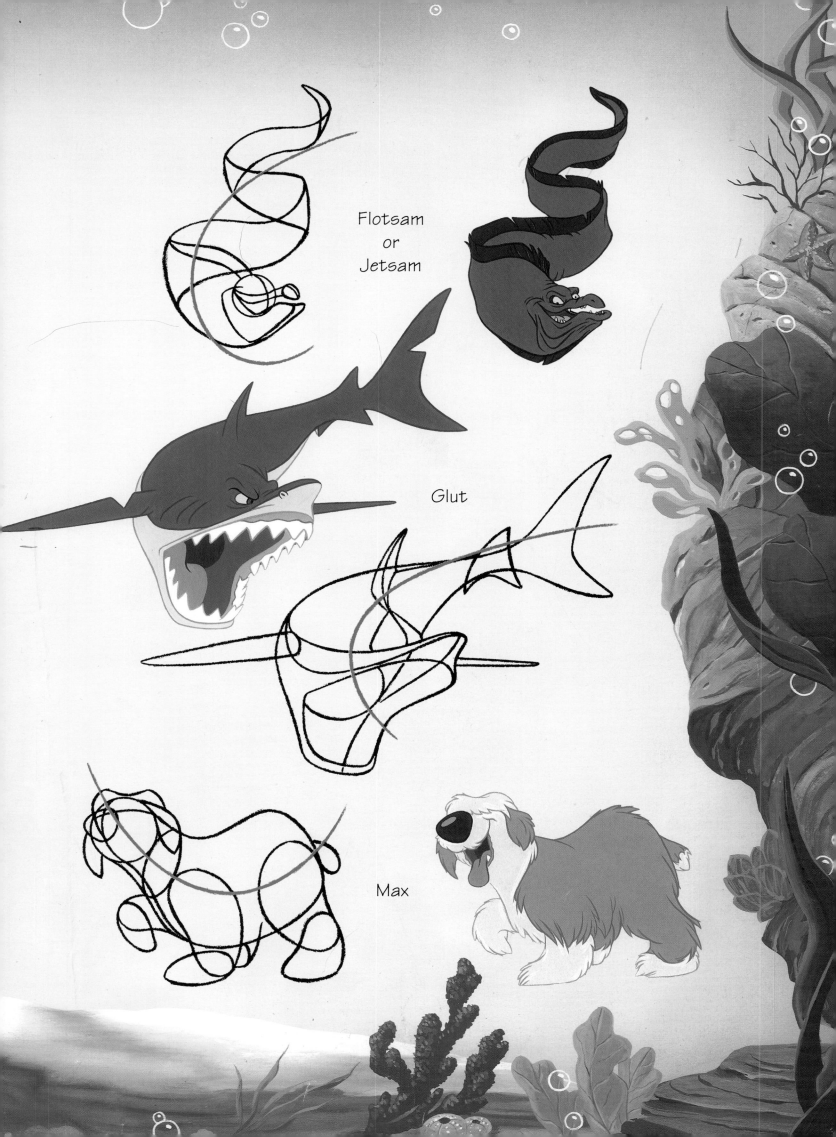

Flotsam
or
Jetsam

Glut

Max